CHURCH AS COMMUNION

An Agreed Statement
by the Second Anglican–Roman Catholic
International Commission
ARCIC II

Published for the Anglican Consultative Council and the
Pontifical Council for Promoting Christian Unity

Published 1991 for the Anglican Consultative Council
157 Waterloo Road, London SE1 8UT
through the Inter-Anglican Publishing Network

and for the Pontifical Council for Promoting Christian Unity,
Vatican City, by the Catholic Truth Society

© Cormac Murphy-O'Connor and Mark Santer, 1991

All rights reserved. No part of this publication may be reproduced or transmitted in any form or by any means, electronic or mechanical, including photocopying, recording, or any information storage and retrieval system, without permission in writing from the copyright owners.

It is not necessary to seek specific permission for the reproduction of extracts from *Church as Communion* amounting in total to not more than five hundred words, provided that an acknowledgement is included as follows:
  Church as Communion: An Agreed Statement by the Second Anglican–Roman Catholic International Commission is copyright © Cormac Murphy-O'Connor and Mark Santer, 1991. Bishop Murphy-O'Connor and Bishop Santer are the Co-Chairmen of ARCIC II.

If it is desired to make more extensive quotation, application should be made to the Co-Chairmen of ARCIC II, c/o the Anglican Consultative Council or the Vatican Pontifical Council for Promoting Christian Unity.

This edition by
Church House Publishing
Church House, Great Smith Street, London SW1P 3NZ
Catholic Truth Society
38-40 Eccleston Square, London SW1V 1PD

ISBN 0 7151 4810 9 (CHP)
ISBN 0 85183 823 5 (CTS)

Printed in England by Tasprint Ltd

PREFACE
by the Co-Chairmen

During the past four years the members of the Anglican–Roman Catholic International Commission have considered the mystery of communion which is given and made visible in the Church. This has not been an easy task, because of the inherent complexity and depth of the mystery. For the same reason, our study cannot be complete or perfect. We have paid particular attention to the sacramentality of the Church; that is, to the Church as a divine gift, grounded in Christ himself and embodied in human history, through which the grace of Christ is mediated for the salvation of humankind. In doing this, we believe that we have laid a necessary foundation for further work on vital topics which were broached by our predecessors in the first Anglican–Roman Catholic International Commission. In particular we look forward to deeper study of the nature of the authority of Christ, the living Word of God, over his Church, and of the means through which he exercises that authority and his people respond to it.

In considering the Church as communion we have drawn upon thinking in both our Churches and in the dialogues with other Christian bodies in which both are engaged. We offer the outcome of our labours not only to our own respective churches, but to all who are concerned with the common search for that full ecclesial unity which we believe to be God's will for all his people. We do this in the hope of study and response.

The members of the Commission have not only been engaged in theological dialogue. Their work and study have been rooted in shared prayer and common life. This in itself has given them a profound experience of communion in Christ; not indeed that full sacramental communion which is our goal, but nevertheless a true foretaste of that fullness of communion for which we pray and strive.

We are painfully aware of the difficulties which still lie in our way. Nevertheless, we are heartened and encouraged by the words of Pope John Paul II and Archbishop Robert Runcie in their Common Declaration of 2 October 1989:

> Against the background of human disunity the arduous journey to Christian unity must be pursued with determination and vigour, whatever obstacles are perceived to block the path. We here solemnly recommit ourselves and those we represent to the restoration of visible unity and full ecclesial communion in the confidence that to seek anything less would be to betray our Lord's intention for the unity of his people.

The Pope and the Archbishop also declared: 'The ecumenical journey is not only about the removal of obstacles but also about the sharing of gifts.' That indeed has been the experience of the members of the Commission. In giving we receive. That is of the essence of communion in Christ.

+CORMAC MURPHY-O'CONNOR

+MARK SANTER

Dublin
6 September 1990

The Status of the Document

The document published here is the work of the Second Anglican–Roman Catholic International Commission (ARCIC II). It is a joint statement of the Commission. The authorities who appointed the Commission have allowed the statement to be published so that it may be widely discussed. It is not an authoritative declaration by the Roman Catholic Church or by the Anglican Communion, who will evaluate the document in order to take a position on it in due time.

CHURCH AS COMMUNION

Introduction

1   Together with other Christians, Anglicans and Roman Catholics are committed to the search for that unity in truth and love for which Christ prayed. Within this context, the purpose of the Anglican–Roman Catholic International Commission is to examine and try to resolve those doctrinal differences which stand in the way of ecclesial communion between Anglicans and Roman Catholics. The *Final Report* of ARCIC I and the publication of ARCIC II's statement on *Salvation and the Church* have contributed to progress in mutual understanding and growing awareness of the need for ecclesial communion. We believe it is time now to reflect more explicitly upon the nature of communion and its constitutive elements. This will enable us to meet the requests that have been made for further clarification of the ecclesiological basis of our work.

2   This statement on communion differs from previous ARCIC reports in that it does not focus specifically on doctrinal questions that have been historically divisive. Nor does it seek to treat all the issues pertaining to the doctrine of the Church. Its purpose is to give substance to the affirmation that Anglicans and Roman Catholics are already in a real though as yet imperfect communion and to enable us to recognise the degree of communion that exists both within and between us.[1] Moreover, we believe that within the perspective of communion the outstanding difficulties that

---

[1] Cf. Common Declaration, Pope John Paul II and the Archbishop of Canterbury, Robert Runcie, 2 October 1989.

remain between us will be more clearly understood and are more likely to be resolved; thus we shall be helped to grow into a more profound communion.

3 There are advantages in adopting the theme of communion in an exploration of the nature of the Church. Communion implies that the Church is a dynamic reality moving towards its fulfilment. Communion embraces both the visible gathering of God's people and its divine life-giving source. We are thus directed to the life of God, Father, Son, and Holy Spirit, the life God wills to share with all people. There is held before us the vision of God's reign over the whole of creation, and of the Church as the firstfruits of humankind which is drawn into that divine life through acceptance of the redemption given in Jesus Christ. Moreover this focus on communion enables us to affirm that which is already realised in the Church, the eucharistic community. It enables us also to acknowledge as a gift of God the good that is present in community life in the world: communion involves rejoicing with those who rejoice and being in solidarity with those who suffer and those who search for meaning in life. To explore the meaning of communion is not only to speak of the Church but also to address the world at the heart of its deepest need, for human beings long for true community in freedom, justice and peace and for the respect of human dignity.

4 Furthermore to understand the Church in terms of communion confronts Christians with the scandal of our divisions. Christian disunity obscures God's invitation to communion for all humankind and makes the Gospel we proclaim harder to hear. But the consideration of communion also enables Christians to recognise that certain yet imperfect communion they already share. Christians of many traditions are coming to acknowledge the central place of communion in their understanding of the nature of the Church and its

unity and mission. This is the communion to the study of which this document is devoted.

5 After a survey of how communion is unfolded in Scripture, we explore the way in which the Church as communion is sacrament of the merciful grace of God for all humankind. Then follows a treatment of the relationship of communion to the apostolicity, catholicity, and holiness of the Church and a consideration of the necessary elements required for unity and ecclesial communion. Finally, we affirm the existing communion between our two churches and outline some of the remaining issues which continue to divide us.

I Communion Unfolded in Scripture

6 The relationship between God and his creation is the fundamental theme of Holy Scripture. The drama of human existence, as expounded in Scripture, consists in the formation, breakdown and renewal of this relationship. The biblical story opens with God establishing this relationship by creating human beings in his image and likeness; God blesses and honours them by inviting them to live in communion both with him and with one another as stewards of his creation. In the unfolding saga of Genesis the disobedience of Adam and Eve undermines both their relation with God and their relation with each other: they hide from God; Adam blames Eve; they are expelled from the garden; their relationship with the rest of creation is distorted. What ensues in Genesis illustrates this recurrent pattern in human history.

7 In the variety of literary styles and theological traditions coming from every period of the long history of the people of Abraham, the books of the Old Testament bear witness to the fact that God wants his people to be in communion with him

and with each other. God's purpose is reaffirmed in covenant with his people. Through Abraham God gives the promise of blessing to all the nations (Gen. 12.1-3). Through Moses God establishes a people as his own possession, a community in a covenant relationship with him (Exodus 19.5-6). In the Promised Land the Temple becomes the place where God chooses to set his name, where he dwells with his people (Deut. 12.5). The prophets consistently denounce the community's faithlessness as threatening this relationship. Nevertheless, God's fidelity remains constant and he promises through the prophets that his promise will be accomplished. Although division and exile follow upon the sins of the chosen people, reconciliation of the scattered people of God will spring from a radical transformation within a new covenant (Jer. 31.31ff). God will raise up a servant to fulfil his purpose of communion and peace for his chosen people and also for all the nations (Isa. 49.6; cf. also Micah 4.1-4).

8 In the fullness of time, God sends his Son, born of a woman, to redeem his people and bring them into a new relationship as his adopted children (cf. Gal. 4.4-5). When Jesus begins his ministry he calls together a band of disciples with whom he shares his mission (Mark 3.14; cf. John 20.21). After Easter they are to be witnesses to his life, teaching, death and resurrection. In the power of the Spirit given at Pentecost they proclaim that God's promises have been fulfilled in Christ. For the Apostolic community the baptism of repentance and faith bestowed in this New Covenant does more than restore that which was lost: by the Spirit believers enter Christ's own communion with the Father. In the eucharist, the memorial of the New Covenant, believers participate in the body and blood of Christ (1 Cor. 11.23-27) and are made one body in him (1 Cor. 10.16-17). It is communion with the Father, through the Son, in the Holy Spirit which constitutes the people of the New Covenant as

the Church, 'a people still linked by spiritual ties to the stock of Abraham'.[2]

9 On Calvary the hideous nature of sin and evil is clearly exposed. In the Cross are found God's judgement upon the world and his gift of reconciliation (2 Cor.5.14-19). Through the Paschal victory all estrangement occasioned by differences of culture, class, privilege and sex is overcome. All those who are united with the death and resurrection of Christ have equal standing before God. Moreover, because Christ is the one in whom and through whom all things are created and reconciled, the proper relationship between humanity and the rest of creation is restored and renewed in him (Col. 1.15-20; Gal. 3.27-29).

10 However, the life of communion is still impaired by human sin (1 Cor. 1.10ff). The failure of Christians to respond to the demands of the Gospel gives rise to divisions among Christians which obscure the Church's witness. The New Testament affirms that there is a constant need for recourse to the repentance and reconciliation offered by Christ through the Church (Matt. 18.15-20; cf. 1 John 1.5-10).

11 In the writings of the New Testament the failures of the disciples and the divisions among them are fully recognised. Nevertheless the reign of God is already perceived as a reality in the world (Mark 1.15; Luke 11.20), even though it will be perfectly realised only in the fullness of the Kingdom of God. Its culmination is described as a feast, 'the wedding supper of the Lamb' (Rev. 19.9), a vivid image of communion deeply rooted in human experience. This feast is spoken of by Jesus in the parables (Matt. 22.1-10), and foreshadowed in the feeding of the multitudes (John 6). The celebration of the eucharist prefigures and provides a foretaste of this messianic

---

[2] Second Vatican Council, *Nostra Aetate*, 4.

banquet (Luke 22.30). In the world to come, such signs will cease since the sacramental order will no longer be needed, for God will be immediately present to his people. They will see him face to face and join in endless praise (Rev. 22.3-4). This will be the perfection of communion.

12   In the New Testament the word *koinonia* (often translated 'communion' or 'fellowship') ties together a number of basic concepts such as unity, life together, sharing and partaking. The basic verbal form means 'to share', 'to participate', 'to have part in', 'to have something in common' or 'to act together'. The noun can signify fellowship or community. It usually signifies a relationship based on participation in a shared reality (e.g. 1 Cor. 10.16). This usage is most explicit in the Johannine writings: 'We proclaim to you what we have seen and heard, so that you also may have fellowship with us. And our fellowship is with the Father and with his Son Jesus Christ' (1 John 1.3; cf. 1 John 1.7).[3]

13   In the New Testament the idea of communion is conveyed in many ways. A variety of words, expressions, and images points to its reality: the people of God (1 Pet. 2.9-10); flock (John 10.14; Acts 20.28-29; 1 Pet. 5.2-4); vine (John 15.5); temple (1 Cor. 3.16-17); bride (Rev. 21.2); body of Christ (1 Cor. 12.27; 1 Cor. 10.17; Rom. 12.4-5; Eph. 1.22-23). All these express a relationship with God and also imply a relationship among the members of the community. The reality to which this variety of images refers is communion, a shared life in Christ (1 Cor. 10.16-17; cf. John 17) which no one image exhaustively describes. This communion is participation in the life of God through Christ in the Holy Spirit, making Christians one with each other.

---

[3] Communion has been treated in many ecumenical documents including the *Final Report* of ARCIC I (Introduction). Cf. also *Communion-Koinonia:* A Study by the Institute for Ecumenical Research, Strasbourg, 1990.

14 It is characteristic of the Apostle Paul to speak of the relationship of believers to their Lord as being 'in Christ' (2. Cor. 5.17; Col. 1.27-28; Gal. 2.20; cf. also John. 15.1-11) and of Christ being in the believer through the indwelling of the Holy Spirit (Rom. 8.1-11). This relationship Paul also affirms in his description of the Church as the one body of Christ. This description is integrally linked with the presence of Christ in the eucharist. Those who share in the supper of the Lord are one body in Christ because they all partake of the one bread (1 Cor. 10.16-17). This description underlines the intimate, organic relationship which exists between the Risen Lord and all those who receive new life through communion with him. Equally it emphasises the organic relationship thus established among the members of the one body, the Church. All who share in the 'holy things' of the sacramental life are made holy through them: because they share in them together they are in communion with each other.

15 The New Testament reflects different dimensions of communion as experienced in the life of the Church in apostolic times.

At the centre of this communion is life with the Father, through Christ, in the Spirit. Through the sending of his Son the living God has revealed that love is at the heart of the divine life. Those who abide in love abide in God and God in them; if we, in communion with him, love one another, he abides in us and his love is perfected in us (cf. 1 John 4.7-21). Through love God communicates his life. He causes those who accept the light of the truth revealed in Christ rather than the darkness of this world to become his children. This is the most profound communion possible for any of his creatures.

Visibly, this communion is entered through baptism and nourished and expressed in the celebration of the eucharist. All who are baptised in the one Spirit into one body are united in the eucharist by this sacramental participation in this same one body (1 Cor. 10.16-17; 12.13). This community of the baptised, devoted to the apostolic teaching, fellowship, breaking of bread and prayer (cf. Acts 2.42), finds its necessary expression in a visible human community. It is a community which suffers with Christ in anticipation of the revelation of his glory (Phil. 3.10; Col. 1.24; 1 Pet. 4.13; Rom. 8.17). Those who are in communion participate in one another's joys and sorrows (Heb. 10.33; 2 Cor. 1.6-7); they serve one another in love (Gal. 5.13) and share together to meet the needs of one another and of the community as a whole. There is a mutual giving and receiving of spiritual and material gifts, not only between individuals but also between communities, on the basis of a fellowship that already exists in Christ (Rom. 15.26-27; 2 Cor. 8.1-15). The integrity and building up of that fellowship require appropriate structure, order and discipline (cf. 1 Cor. 11.17-34 and the Pastoral Epistles *passim*).

Communion will reach its fulfilment when God will be all in all (1 Cor. 15.28). It is the will of God for the whole creation that all things should be brought to ultimate unity and communion in Christ (Eph. 1.10; Col. 1.19-20).

Already in the New Testament these different dimensions of communion are discernible, together with a striving towards their ever more faithful realisation.

II Communion: Sacramentality and the Church

16   God's purpose is to bring all people into communion with himself within a transformed creation (cf. Rom. 8.19-21). To accomplish this the eternal Word became incarnate. The life and ministry of Jesus Christ definitively manifested the restored humanity God intends. By who he was, by what he taught, and by what he accomplished through the Cross and resurrection, he became the sign, the instrument, and the

firstfruits of God's purpose for the whole of creation (Col. 1.15-17). As the new Adam, the Risen Lord is the beginning and guarantor of this transformation. Through this transformation, alienation is overcome by communion, both between human beings and above all between them and God. These two dimensions of communion are inseparable. This is the mystery of Christ (Eph. 2.11–3.12).

17 Communion with God through Christ is constantly established and renewed through the power of the Holy Spirit. By the power of the Spirit, the incomparable riches of God's grace are made present for all time through the Church. Those who are reconciled to God form 'one body in Christ and are individually members one of another' (Rom. 12.5). By the action of the same Spirit, believers are baptised into the one Body (1 Cor. 12.13) and in the breaking of the bread they also participate in that one Body (1 Cor. 10.16-17; 11.23-29). Thus the Church 'which is Christ's body, the fullness of him who fills all in all', reveals and embodies 'the mystery of Christ' (cf. Eph. 1.23; 3.4, 8-11). It is therefore itself rightly described as a visible sign which both points to and embodies our communion with God and with one another; as an instrument through which God effects this communion; and as a foretaste of the fullness of communion to be consummated when Christ is all in all. It is a 'mystery' or 'sacrament'.

18 The Church as communion of believers with God and with each other is a sign of the new humanity God is creating and a pledge of the continuing work of the Holy Spirit. Its vocation is to embody and reveal the redemptive power of the Gospel, signifying reconciliation received through faith and participation in the new life in Christ. The Church is the sign of what God has done in Christ, is continuing to do in those who serve him, and wills to do for all humanity. It is the sign of God's abiding presence, and of his eternal faithfulness to his

promises, for in it Christ is ever present and active through the Spirit. It is the community where the redemptive work of Jesus Christ has been recognised and received, and is therefore being made known to the world. Because Christ has overcome all the barriers of division created by human sin, it is the mission of the Church as God's servant to enter into the struggle to end those divisions (cf. Eph. 2.14-18; 5.1-2).

19 The Holy Spirit uses the Church as the means through which the Word of God is proclaimed afresh, the sacraments are celebrated, and the people of God receive pastoral oversight, so that the life of the Gospel is manifested in the life of its members. The Church is both the sign of salvation in Christ, for to be saved is to be brought into communion with God through him, and at the same time the instrument of salvation, as the community through which this salvation is offered and received. This is what is meant when the Church is described as an 'effective sign', given by God in the face of human sinfulness, division and alienation.[4]

20 Human sinfulness and Christian division obscure this sign. However, Christ's promise of his abiding presence in the midst of his people (Matt. 18.20; 28.20) gives the assurance that the Church will not cease to be this effective sign. In spite of the frailty and sinfulness of its members, Christ promises

[4] The language of 'effective sign' and 'instrument' is known to Anglicans in the Catechism of the Book of Common Prayer and in the Articles of Religion, in which baptism and the eucharist are said to be 'not only a sign... but rather... a sacrament', 'sure witnesses, and effectual signs of grace', 'as a means whereby we receive' grace, 'as by an instrument', and which 'be effectual because of Christ's institution and promise' (The Catechism; Articles 25, 26, 27, 28). For the Roman Catholic Church, similarly, instrumental language was largely developed in relation to the sacraments rather than the Church. But reflection on the mystery of Christ and the Church led to the development of its self-understanding in terms of itself being 'in Christ... in the nature of sacrament – a sign and instrument, that is, of communion with God and of unity among all people', and 'as the universal sacrament of salvation' *(Lumen Gentium* 1, 48).

that the powers of destruction will never prevail against it (Matt. 16.18).

21 Paradoxically it is pre-eminently in its weakness, suffering and poverty that the Church becomes the sign of the efficacy of God's grace (cf. 2 Cor. 12.9; 4.7-12). It is also paradoxical that the quality of holiness is rightly attributed to the Church, a community of sinners. The power of God to sanctify the Church is revealed in the scandal of the Cross where Christ in his love gave himself for the Church so that it might be presented to him without spot or wrinkle, holy and without blemish (Eph. 5.26-27). God was in Christ reconciling the world to himself, making him who knew no sin to be sin for us so that in him we might become the righteousness of God (cf. 2 Cor. 5.19-21).

22 The communion of the Church demonstrates that Christ has broken down the dividing wall of hostility, so as to create a single new humanity reconciled to God in one body by the Cross (cf. Eph. 2.14-16). Confessing that their communion signifies God's purpose for the whole human race, the members of the Church are called to give themselves in loving witness and service to their fellow human beings.

This service is focused principally in the proclaiming of the Gospel in obedience to the command of Christ. Having received this call, the Church has been entrusted with the stewardship of the means of grace and with the message of salvation. In the power of Christ's presence through the Spirit it is caught up in the saving mission of Christ. The mandate given to the Church to bring salvation to all the nations constitutes its unique mission. In this way the Church not only signifies the new humanity willed by God and inaugurated by Christ. It is itself an instrument of the Holy Spirit in the extension of salvation to all human beings in all their needs and circumstances to the end of time. To speak of the Church as sacrament is to affirm that in and through the communion of all those who confess Jesus Christ and who live according to their confession, God realises his plan of salvation for all the world. This is not to say that God's saving work is limited to those who confess Christ explicitly. By God's gift of the same Spirit who was at work in the earthly ministry of Christ Jesus, the Church plays its part in bringing his work to its fulfilment.

23   To be united with Christ in the fulfilment of his ministry for the salvation of the world is to share his will that the Church be one, not only for the credibility of the Church's witness and for the effectiveness of its mission, but supremely for the glorification of the Father. God will be truly glorified when all peoples with their rich diversity will be fully united in one communion of love. Our present communion with God and with each other in the Holy Spirit is a pledge and foretaste here and now of the ultimate fulfilment of God's purpose for all, as proclaimed in the vision of 'a great multitude which none could number, from every nation, from all tribes and peoples and tongues . . . crying out with a loud voice, 'Salvation belongs to our God who sits upon the throne, and to the Lamb!' (Rev. 7.9-10).

24   The sacramental nature of the Church as sign, instrument, and foretaste of communion is especially manifest in the common celebration of the eucharist. Here, celebrating the memorial of the Lord and partaking of his body and blood, the Church points to the origin of its communion in Christ, himself in communion with the Father; it experiences that communion in a visible fellowship; it anticipates the fullness of the communion in the Kingdom; it is sent out to realise, manifest and extend that communion in the world.

III Communion: Apostolicity, Catholicity and Holiness

25 The Church points to its source and mission when it confesses in the Creed, 'We believe in one holy catholic and apostolic Church'. It is because the Church is built up by the Spirit upon the foundation of the life, death and resurrection of Christ as these have been witnessed and transmitted by the apostles that the Church is called *apostolic*. It is also called apostolic because it is equipped for its mission by sharing in the apostolic mandate.

26 The content of the faith is the truth of Christ Jesus as it has been transmitted through the apostles. This God-given deposit of faith cannot be dissociated from the gift of the Holy Spirit. Central to the mission of the Spirit is the safeguarding and quickening of the memory of the teaching and work of Christ and of his exaltation, of which the apostolic community was the first witness. To safeguard the authenticity of its memory the Church was led to acknowledge the canon of Scripture as both test and norm. But the quickening of its memory requires more than the repetition of the words of Scripture. It is achieved under the guidance of the Holy Spirit by the unfolding of revealed truth as it is in Jesus Christ. According to the Johannine gospel the mission of the Holy Spirit is intimately linked with all that Christ Jesus said, did and accomplished. Christ promised that the Father will send the Holy Spirit in his name to teach the disciples all things and to bring to remembrance all that he has said (cf. John 14.26). To keep alive the memory of Christ means to remain faithful to all that we know of him through the apostolic community.

27 Such faithfulness must be realised in daily life. Consequently in every age and culture authentic faithfulness

is expressed in new ways and by fresh insights through which the understanding of the apostolic preaching is enriched. Thus the Gospel is not transmitted solely as a text. The living Word of God, together with the Spirit, communicates God's invitation to communion to the whole of his world in every age. This dynamic process constitutes what is called the living tradition, the living memory of the Church. Without this the faithful transmission of the Gospel is impossible.

28 The living memory of the mystery of Christ is present and active within the Church as a whole; it is at work in the constant confession and celebration of the apostolic faith and in the insights, emphases and perspectives of faithful members of the Church. And since faith seeks understanding, this includes an examination of the very foundations of faith. As the social setting of the Christian community changes, so the questions and challenges posed both from within and from without the Church are never entirely the same. Even within the period covered by the New Testament this process is evident when new images and fresh language are used to express the faith as it is handed on in changing cultural contexts.

29 If the Church is to remain faithfully rooted and grounded in the living truth and is to confess it with relevance, then it will need to develop new expressions of the faith. Diversity of cultures may often elicit a diversity in the expression of the one Gospel; within the same community distinct perceptions and practices arise. Nevertheless these must remain faithful to the tradition received from the apostles (cf. Jude 3). Since the Holy Spirit is given to all the people of God, it is within the Church as a whole, individuals as well as communities, that the living memory of the faith is active. All authentic insights and perceptions, therefore, have their place within the life and faith of the whole Church, the temple of the Holy Spirit.

30   Tensions inevitably appear. Some are creative of healthy development. Some may cause a loss of continuity with apostolic tradition, disruption within the community, estrangement from other parts of the Church. Within the history of Christianity, some diversities have become differences that have led to such conflict that ecclesial communion has been severed. Whenever differences become embodied in separated ecclesial communities, so that Christians are no longer able to receive and pass on the truth within the one community of faith, communion is impoverished and the living memory of the Church is affected. As Christians grow apart, complementary aspects of the one truth are sometimes perceived as mutually incompatible. Nevertheless the Church is sustained by Christ's promise of its perseverance in the truth (cf. Matt. 16.18), even though its unity and peace are constantly vulnerable. The ultimate God-given safeguard for this assurance is the action of the Spirit in preserving the living memory of Christ.

31   This memory, realised and freshly expressed in every age and culture, constitutes the apostolic tradition of the Church. In recognising the canon of Scripture as the normative record of the revelation of God, the Church sealed as authoritative its accceptance of the transmitted memory of the apostolic community. This is summarised and embodied in the creeds. The Holy Spirit makes this tradition a living reality which is perpetually celebrated and proclaimed by word and sacrament, pre-eminently in the eucharistic memorial of the once-for-all sacrifice of Christ, in which the Scriptures have always been read. Thus the apostolic tradition is fundamental to the Church's communion which spans time and space, linking the present to past and future generations of Christians.

32   Responsibility for the maintenance of the apostolic faith is shared by the whole people of God. Every Christian has a part in this responsibility. The task of those entrusted with oversight, acting in the name of Christ, is to foster the promptings of the Spirit and to keep the community within the bounds of the apostolic faith, to sustain and promote the Church's mission, by preaching, explaining and applying its truth. In responding to the insights of the community, and of the individual Christian, whose conscience is also moulded by the same Spirit, those exercising oversight seek to discern what is the mind of Christ. Discernment involves both heeding and sifting in order to assist the people of God in understanding, articulating and applying their faith. Sometimes an authoritative expression has to be given to the insights and convictions of the faithful. The community actively responds to the teaching of the ordained ministry, and when, under the guidance of the Spirit, it recognises the apostolic faith, it assimilates its content into its life.

33   Succession in the episcopal ministry is intended to assure each community that its faith is indeed the apostolic faith, received and transmitted from apostolic times. Further, by means of the communion among those entrusted with the episcopal ministry the whole Church is made aware of the perceptions and concerns of the local churches: at the same time the local churches are enabled to maintain their place and particular character within the communion of all the churches.

34   In the Creeds the Church has always confessed its *catholicity:* 'I believe in . . . the holy catholic Church'. It gets this title from the fact that by its nature it is to be scattered throughout the world, from one end of the earth to the other, from one age to the next. The Church is also catholic because its mission is to teach universally and without omission all that

has been revealed by God for the salvation and fulfilment of humankind; and also because its vocation is to unite in one eucharistic fellowship men and women of every race, culture and social condition in every generation. Because it is the fruit of the work of Christ upon the cross, destroying all barriers of division, making Jews and Gentiles one holy people, both having access to the one Father by the one Spirit (cf. Eph. 2.14-18), the Church is catholic.

35 In the mystery of his will God intends the Church to be the re-creation in Christ Jesus of all the richness of human diversity that sin turns into division and strife (cf. Eph. 1.9-10). In so far as this re-creation is authentically demonstrated in its life, the Church is a sign of hope to a divided world that longs for peace and harmony. It is the grace and Gospel of God that brings together this human diversity without stifling or destroying it; the Church's catholicity expresses the depth of the wisdom of the Creator. Human beings were created by God in his love with such diversity in order that they might participate in that love by sharing with one another both what they have and what they are, thus enriching each other in their mutual communion.

36 Throughout its history the Church has been called to demonstrate that salvation is not restricted to particular cultures. This is evident in the variety of liturgies and forms of spirituality, in the variety of disciplines and ways of exercising authority, in the variety of theological approaches, and even in the variety of theological expressions of the same doctrine. These varieties complement one another, showing that, as the result of communion with God in Christ, diversity does not lead to division; on the contrary, it serves to bring glory to God for the munificence of his gifts. Thus the Church in its catholicity is the place where God brings glory to his name through the communion of those he created in his own

image and likeness, so diverse yet profoundly one. At every eucharistic celebration of Christian communities dispersed throughout the world, in their variety of cultures, languages, social and political contexts, it is the same one and indivisible body of Christ reconciling divided humanity that is offered to believers. In this way the eucharist is the sacrament of the Church's catholicity in which God is glorified.

37 In the eucharist the Church also manifests its solidarity with the whole of humanity. This is given expression in intercession and thanksgiving, and in the sending out of the people of God to serve and to proclaim the message of salvation to the world. The Church's concern for the poor and oppressed is not peripheral but belongs to the very heart of its mission (cf. 2 Cor. 8.1-9).

Moreover, for the Church effectively to carry out its ministry of reconciliation, it is necessary that its members and communities display in their common life the fruits of Christ's reconciling work. As long as Christians are divided, they do not fully manifest the catholic nature of the Church.

38 Catholicity is inseparable from holiness, as is evident from the early liturgical traditions which often speak of 'the holy catholic church', and from early forms of the Creed which include the words 'We believe in the Holy Spirit in the holy Catholic Church'. The Church is *holy* because it is 'God's special possession'(1 Pet. 2.9-10), endowed with his Spirit (Eph. 2.21-22), and it is his special possession since it is there that 'the mystery of his will, according to his good pleasure' is realised, 'to bring all things in heaven and on earth together under one head, Christ' (Eph. 1.9-10).

Being set apart as God's special possession means that the Church is the communion of those who seek to be perfect as their Heavenly Father is perfect (Matt. 5.48). This implies a life in communion with Christ, a life of compassion, love and righteousness. The holiness of the Church does not mean that it is to be cut off from the world (John 17.15ff). Its vocation is to be, through its holiness, salt of the earth, light to the world (Matt. 5.13-16). In this way the Church declares the praises of him who called his people out of darkness into his marvellous light (cf. 1 Pet. 2.9).

39 The catholicity of God's purpose requires that all the diverse gifts and graces given by God to sanctify his people should find their proper place in the Church. Every Christian is called to be consecrated to the life and service of the communion (1 Pet. 4.10ff; 1 Cor. 12.4ff). And what is true of the individual is equally true of the local churches. Communion with other local churches is essential to the integrity of the self-understanding of each local church, precisely because of its catholicity. Life in self-sufficient isolation, which rejects the enrichment coming from other local churches as well as the sharing with them of gifts and resources, spiritual as well as material, is the denial of its very being. It is the particular ministry of oversight to affirm and order the diverse gifts and graces of individuals and communities; to effect and embody the unity of the local church and its unity with the wider communion of the churches. By the example of their lives those who bear oversight are to witness to the holiness of the Church and in their ministry foster holiness amongst its members.

Amid all the diversity that the catholicity intended by God implies, the Church's unity and coherence are maintained by the common confession of the one apostolic faith, a shared sacramental life, a common ministry of oversight, and joint ways of reaching decisions and giving authoritative teaching.

40 The catholicity of the Church is threatened, in the first place, when the apostolic faith is distorted or denied within

the community. It is also threatened whenever the faith is obscured by attitudes and behaviour in the Church which are not in accord with its calling to be the holy people of God, drawn together by the Spirit to live in communion. Just as the Church has to distinguish between tolerable and intolerable diversity in the expression of the apostolic faith, so in the area of life and practice the Church has to discover what is constructive and what is disruptive of its own communion. Catholicity and holiness are also impaired when the Church fails to confront the causes of injustice and oppression which tear humanity apart or when it fails to hear the cries of those calling for sustenance, respect, peace and freedom.

41 When the Creed speaks of the Church as holy, catholic and apostolic, it does not mean that these attributes are distinct and unrelated. On the contrary, they are so interwoven that there cannot be one without the others. The holiness of the Church reflects the mission of the Spirit of God in Christ, the Holy One of God, made known to all the world through the apostolic teaching. Catholicity is the realisation of the Church's proclamation of the fullness of the Gospel to every nation throughout the ages. Apostolicity unites the Church of all generations and in every place with the once-for-all sacrifice and resurrection of Christ, where God's holy love was supremely demonstrated.

IV Unity and Ecclesial Communion

42 The Church, since apostolic times, has always included belief in its unity among the articles of faith (e.g. 1 Cor. 12.12ff; Eph. 4.4-6). Because there is only one Lord, with whom we are called to have communion in the one Spirit, God has given his Church one gospel, one faith, one baptism, one eucharist, and one apostolic ministry through which Christ continues to feed and guide his flock.

43   For a Christian the life of *communion* means sharing in the divine life, being united with the Father, through his Son, in the Holy Spirit, and consequently to be in fellowship with all those who share in the same gift of eternal life. This is a spiritual communion in which the reality of the life of the world to come is already present. But it is inadequate to speak only of an invisible spiritual unity as the fulfilment of Christ's will for the Church; the profound communion fashioned by the Spirit requires visible expression. The purpose of the visible ecclesial community is to embody and promote this spiritual communion with God (cf. paras. 16-24).

For a local community to be *a communion* means that it is a gathering of the baptised brought together by the apostolic preaching, confessing the one faith, celebrating the one eucharist, and led by an apostolic ministry. This implies that this local church is in communion with all Christian communities in which the essential constitutive elements of ecclesial life are present.

For all the local churches to be *together in communion,* the one visible communion which God wills, it is required that all the essential constitutive elements of ecclesial communion are present and mutually recognised in each of them. Thus the visible communion between these churches is complete and their ministers are in communion with each other. This does not necessitate precisely the same canonical ordering: diversity of canonical structures is part of the acceptable diversity which enriches the one communion of all the churches.

44   The *constitutive elements* essential for the visible communion of the Church are derived from and subordinate to the common confession of Jesus Christ as Lord. In the picture of the Jerusalem church in the Acts of the Apostles we can already see in nascent form certain necessary elements of

ecclesial communion which must be present in the Church in every age (cf. para. 15).

45 In the light of all that we have said about communion it is now possible to describe what constitutes ecclesial communion. It is rooted in the confession of the one apostolic faith, revealed in the Scriptures, and set forth in the Creeds. It is founded upon one baptism. The one celebration of the eucharist is its pre-eminent expression and focus. It necessarily finds expression in shared commitment to the mission entrusted by Christ to his Church. It is a life of shared concern for one another in mutual forbearance, submission, gentleness and love; in the placing of the interests of others above the interests of self; in making room for each other in the body of Christ; in solidarity with the poor and the powerless; and in the sharing of gifts both material and spiritual (cf. Acts 2.44). Also constitutive of life in communion is acceptance of the same basic moral values, the sharing of the same vision of humanity created in the image of God and recreated in Christ, and the common confession of the one hope in the final consummation of the Kingdom of God.

For the nurture and growth of this communion, Christ the Lord has provided a ministry of oversight, the fullness of which is entrusted to the episcopate, which has the responsibility of maintaining and expressing the unity of the churches (cf. paras. 33 and 39 and *The Final Report,* Ministry and Ordination). By shepherding, teaching and the celebration of the sacraments, especially the eucharist, this ministry holds believers together in the communion of the local church and in the wider communion of all the churches (cf. para. 39). This ministry of oversight has both collegial and primatial dimensions. It is grounded in the life of the community and is open to the community's participation in the discovery of God's will. It is exercised so that unity and communion are expressed, preserved and fostered at every level – locally, regionally and universally. In the context of the communion of all the churches the episcopal ministry of a universal primate finds its role as the visible focus of unity.

Throughout history different means have been used to express, preserve and foster this communion between bishops: the participation of bishops of neighbouring sees in episcopal ordinations; prayer for bishops of other dioceses in the liturgy; exchanges of episcopal letters. Local churches recognised the necessity of maintaining communion with the principal sees, particularly with the See of Rome. The practice of holding synods or councils, local, provincial, ecumenical, arose from the need to maintain unity in the one apostolic faith (cf. *The Final Report,* Authority in the Church, I.19-23, II.12).

46 All these interrelated elements and facets belong to the visible communion of the universal Church. Although their possession cannot guarantee the constant fidelity of Christians, neither can the Church dispense with them. They need to be present in order for one local church to recognise another canonically. This does not mean that a community in which they are present expresses them fully in its life.

47 Christians can never acquiesce with complacency in disunity without impairing further their communion with God. As separated churches grow towards ecclesial communion it is essential to recognise the profound measure of communion they already share through participation in spiritual communion with God and through those elements of a visible communion of shared faith and sacramental life they can already recognise in one another. If some element or important facet of visible communion is judged to be lacking,

the communion between them, though it may be real, is incomplete.

48 Within the pilgrim Church on earth, even when it enjoys complete ecclesial communion, Christians will be obliged to seek even deeper communion with God and one another. This is also expressed through faith in the 'Communion of Saints', whereby the Church declares its conviction that the eucharistic community on earth is itself a participation in a larger communion which includes the martyrs and confessors and all who have fallen asleep in Christ throughout the ages. The perfection of full communion will only be reached in the fullness of the Kingdom of God.

V Communion Between Anglicans and Roman Catholics

49 The convictions which this Commission believes that Anglicans and Roman Catholics share concerning the nature of communion challenge both our churches to move forward together towards visible unity and ecclesial communion. Progress in mutual understanding has been achieved. There exists a significant degree of doctrinal agreement between our two communions even upon subjects which previously divided us. In spite of past estrangements, Anglicans and Roman Catholics now enjoy a better understanding of their long-standing shared inheritance. This new understanding enables them to recognise in each other's church a true affinity.

50 Thus we already share in the communion founded upon the saving life and work of Christ and his continuing presence through the Holy Spirit. This was acknowledged jointly in the Common Declaration of Pope John Paul II and Archbishop Robert Runcie of 2 October 1989.

We also urge our clergy and faithful not to neglect or undervalue that certain yet imperfect communion we already share. This communion already shared is grounded in faith in God our Father, in our Lord Jesus Christ, and in the Holy Spirit; our common baptism into Christ; our sharing of the Holy Scriptures, of the Apostles' and Nicene Creeds; the Chalcedonian definition and the teaching of the Fathers; our common Christian inheritance for many centuries. This communion should be cherished and guarded as we seek to grow into the fuller communion Christ wills. Even in the years of our separation we have been able to recognise gifts of the Spirit in each other. The ecumenical journey is not only about the removal of obstacles but also about the sharing of gifts.

51   One of the most important ways in which there has already been a sharing of gifts is in spirituality and worship. Roman Catholics and Anglicans now frequently pray together. Alongside common participation in public worship and in private prayer, members of both churches draw from a common treasury of spiritual writing and direction. There has been a notable convergence in our patterns of liturgy, especially in that of the eucharist. The same lectionary is used by both churches in many countries. We now agree on the use of the vernacular language in public worship. We agree also that communion in both kinds is the appropriate mode of administration of the eucharist. In some circumstances, buildings are shared.

52   In some areas there is collaboration in Christian education and in service to local communities. For a number of years, Roman Catholic and Anglican scholars have worked together in universities and other academic institutions. There is closer co-operation in ministerial formation and between parochial clergy and religious communities. The responsibility for the pastoral care of inter-church families is now increasingly entrusted to both churches. Meetings of

Roman Catholic and Anglican bishops are becoming customary, engendering mutual understanding and confidence. This often results in joint witness, practical action and common statements on social and moral issues. The growing measure of ecclesial communion experienced in these ways is the fruit of the communion we share with the Father, through the Son, in the Holy Spirit.

53 We cannot, however, ignore the effects of our centuries of separation. Such separation has inevitably led to the growth of divergent patterns of authority accompanied by changes in perceptions and practices. The differences between us are not only theological. Anglicans and Roman Catholics have now inherited different cultural traditions. Such differences in communities which have become isolated from one another have sometimes led to distortions in the popular perceptions which members of one church have of the other. As a result visible unity may be viewed as undesirable or even unattainable. However, a closer examination of the developments which have taken place in our different communities shows that these developments, when held in complementarity, can contribute to a fuller understanding of communion.

54 In recent years each communion has learnt from its own and each other's experiences, as well as through contact with other churches. Since the Second Vatican Council, the principle of collegiality and the need to adapt to local cultural conditions have been more clearly recognised by the Roman Catholic Church than before. Developing liturgical diversity, the increasing exercise of provincial autonomy, and the growing appreciation of the universal nature of the Church have led Anglicans to develop organs of consultation and unity within their own communion. These developments remind us of the significance of mutual support and criticism,

as together we seek to understand ecclesial communion and to achieve it.

55 Developments in the understanding of the theology of communion in each of our churches have provided the background for the Commission's reflections on the nature of communion. This Statement intends to be faithful to the doctrinal formulations to which Anglicans and Roman Catholics are each committed without providing an exhaustive treatment of the doctrine of the Church.

56 Grave obstacles from the past and of recent origin must not lead us into thinking that there is no further room for growth towards fuller communion. It is clear to the Commission, as we conclude this document, that, despite continuing obstacles, our two Communions agree in their understanding of the Church as communion. Despite our distinct historical experiences, this firm basis should encourage us to proceed to examine our continuing differences.

57 Our approach to the unresolved matters we must now face together will be shaped by the agreed understanding of communion we have elaborated.

An appreciation both of the existing degree of communion between Anglicans and Roman Catholics as well as the complete ecclesial communion to which we are called will provide a context for the discussion of the long-standing problem of the reconciliation of ministries which forms part of ARCIC II's mandate. This will build upon ARCIC I's work on Ministry and Ordination, which provides a new context for discussion of the consequences of the Bull *Apostolicae Curae* (1896).

In the light of our agreement we must also address the present and future implications of the ordination of women to the priesthood and episcopate in those Anglican provinces which consider this to be a legitimate development within the catholic and apostolic tradition. The Lambeth Conference of 1988, while resolving that 'each Province respect the decision and attitudes of other Provinces in the ordination or consecration of women to the episcopate', also stressed the importance of 'maintaining the highest possible degree of communion with the Provinces that differ' (Resolution 1, 1).

Writing to the Archbishop of Canterbury shortly after the Lambeth Conference, Pope John Paul II said of the ordination of women that 'The Catholic Church, like the Orthodox Church and the Ancient Oriental Churches, is firmly opposed to this development, viewing it as a break with Tradition of a kind we have no competence to authorise.' Referring to ARCIC's work in the reconciliation of ministries the Pope said that 'the ordination of women to the priesthood in some provinces of the Anglican Communion, together with the recognition of the right of individual provinces to proceed with the ordination of women to the episcopacy appears to preempt this study and effectively block the path to the mutual recognition of ministries' (Letter of Pope John Paul II to the Archbishop of Canterbury, 8 December 1988).

Another area which the Commission is currently engaged in studying is that of moral issues. Our distinct cultural inheritances have sometimes led us to treat of moral questions in different ways. Our study will explore the moral dimension of Christian life and seek to explain and assess its significance for communion as well as the importance of agreement or difference on particular moral questions.

It is evident that the above issues are closely connected with the question of authority. We continue to believe that an agreed understanding of the Church as communion is the appropriate context in which to continue the study of authority in the Church begun by ARCIC I. Further study will be needed of episcopal authority, particularly of universal primacy, and of the office of the Bishop of Rome; of the question of provincial autonomy in the Anglican Communion; and the role of the laity in decision-making within the Church. This work will take into account the response of the Lambeth Conference 1988 and the response of the Roman Catholic Church to the *Final Report* of ARCIC I.

58 Serious as these remaining obstacles may seem, we should not overlook the extent of the communion already existing between our two churches, which we have described in the last part of this Statement. Indeed, awareness of this fact will help us to bear the pain of our differences without complacency or despair. It should encourage Anglicans and Roman Catholics locally to search for further steps by which concrete expression can be given to this communion which we share. Paradoxically, the closer we draw together the more acutely we feel those differences which remain. The forbearance and generosity with which we seek to resolve these remaining differences will testify to the character of the fuller communion for which we strive. Together with all Christians, Anglicans and Roman Catholics are called by God to continue to pursue the goal of complete communion of faith and sacramental life. This call we must obey until all come into the fullness of that Divine Presence, to whom, Father, Son, and Holy Spirit, be ascribed all honour, thanksgiving and praise to the ages of ages. Amen.

MEMBERS OF THE COMMISSION

Anglican Members

The Rt Revd Mark Santer, Bishop of Birmingham, UK
(*Co-Chairman*)

The Rt Revd John Baycroft, Suffragan Bishop of Ottawa, Canada

The Rt Revd E.D. Cameron, Assistant Bishop, Diocese of Sydney, Australia

The Revd Professor Henry Chadwick, Master of Peterhouse, Cambridge, UK (until 1989)

The Revd Julian Charley, Priest-in-charge of Great Malvern, UK

The Revd Dr Kortright Davis, Professor of Theology, Howard University Divinity School, Washington, DC, USA

The Rt Revd Dr David M. Gitari, Bishop of Mount Kenya East, Kenya (until 1989)

The Revd Canon Christopher Hill, Canon Residentiary of St Paul's Cathedral, London, UK (from 1990, previously Anglican Co-Secretary)

The Revd Professor Oliver O'Donovan, Regius Professor of Moral and Pastoral Theology, University of Oxford, UK

The Revd Professor John Pobee, Programme on Ecumenical Theological Education, World Council of Churches, Geneva, Switzerland

Dr Mary Tanner, Secretary Designate, Council for Christian Unity of the General Synod of the Church of England, London, UK

The Rt Revd Arthur A. Vogel, Retired Bishop of West Missouri, USA

The Revd Professor J. Robert Wright, Professor of Church History, General Theological Seminary, New York, USA

SECRETARY

The Revd Canon Stephen Platten, Archbishop of Canterbury's Secretary for Ecumenical Affairs, London, UK (from 1990)

Roman Catholic Members

The Rt Revd Cormac Murphy-O'Connor, Bishop of Arundel and Brighton, UK *(Co-Chairman)*

The Revd Fr Abraham Adappur, SJ, Staff Member, Lumen Institute, Cochin, India (until 1988)

The Revd Fr Peter Damian Akpunonu, Rector, Catholic Institute of West Africa, Port Harcourt, Nigeria

Sister Dr Mary Cecily Boulding, OP, Lecturer in Systematic Theology, Ushaw College, Durham, UK

The Most Revd Peter Butelezi, OMI, Archbishop of Bloemfontein, South Africa

The Rt Revd Pierre Duprey, Titular Bishop of Thibare, Secretary, Pontifical Council for Promoting Christian Unity, Vatican City

The Rt Revd Raymond W. Lessard, Bishop of Savannah, USA

The Revd Brendan Soane, Spiritual Director, Pontifical Beda College, Rome, Italy

The Revd Fr John Thornhill, SM, Lecturer in Systematic Theology, Catholic Theological Union, Hunters Hill, NSW, Australia

The Revd Fr Jean M.R. Tillard, OP, Professor of Dogmatic Theology, Dominican Faculty of Theology, Ottawa, Canada

The Most Revd Bernard J. Wallace, Bishop of Rockhampton, Australia (1986-88)

The Revd Dr Edward Yarnold, SJ, Tutor in Theology, Campion Hall, Oxford, UK

SECRETARY

The Very Revd Mgr Kevin McDonald, Staff Member, Pontifical Council for Promoting Christian Unity, The Vatican (from 1985)

World Council of Churches Observer

The Revd Dr. Gunther Gassmann, Director, Faith and Order Commission, WCC, Geneva, Switzerland

Church as Communion is the second Agreed Statement of the second Anglican–Roman Catholic International Commission. It follows *Salvation and the Church* published in 1987. The Commission has taken four years to complete its study. It met near Rome (1987), in Edinburgh (1988), in Venice (1989) and finally in Dublin (1990).

Unlike previous Agreed Statements of either ARCIC I or ARCIC II, this document does not touch upon issues which have historically divided the two Churches. But behind many past divisions there has lurked the mutual suspicion that Anglicans and Roman Catholics have divergent understandings of the Church. This is also true of contemporary issues between the Churches such as the ordination of women and questions relating to authority. Official requests have come from both sides for expansion of what ARCIC I and II have already said about the Church as communion.

This Statement does not claim to be a complete agreement about the Church. It states a common understanding of the shared life with God and with our fellow human beings which is the mystery of communion - the Church. This is a necessary foundation for further work on authority, and ordination and ministry, already begun by ARCIC I, and to new work on moral and ethical issues.

The Statement also shows the degree to which Anglicans and Roman Catholics *already* share a true but imperfect communion.

CATHOLIC TRUTH
SOCIETY

CHURCH HOUSE
PUBLISHING

£1.25

ISBN 0 85183 823 5 (CTS)
ISBN 0 7151 4810 9 (CHP)

**Jointly published by
Catholic Truth Society and Church House Publishing**

SALVATION AND THE CHURCH
WITH COMMENTARY AND STUDY GUIDE

The first Agreed Statement of ARCIC II. The text is printed in parallel with a commentary by M. Cecily Boulding OP and Timothy Bradshaw. Topics for discussion are provided, giving the basis of five studies. *Published for the English Anglican–Roman Catholic Committee.*

CTS ISBN 0 85183 787 5
CHP ISBN 0 7151 4792 7 £2.00

The separate publication *Salvation and the Church* (text only) is no longer available.

ONE IN HOPE

The Archbishop of Canterbury's Visit to Pope John Paul II
29 September – 2 October 1989

A pictorial and textual record, giving the full text of the addresses of the Pope and the Archbishop including the Common Declaration of 2 October 1989. Colour photographs by Arturo Mari of *l'Osservatore Romano*.

CTS ISBN 0 85183 793 X
CHP ISBN 0 7151 4794 3 £2.50

Prices are correct as at January 1991